"Finally, a clear guide to comm shows us simply and clearly the words to create, heal, and bless. ... is delicious food for the soul!"

EDWENE GAINES,
Bestselling Author of *The Four Spiritual Laws of Prosperity*

"With so many people hungering and thirsting for a positive alternative to negative religious experiences, *How to Speak Unity* is a perfect introduction to Unity's practical, spiritual teachings that empower abundant and meaningful living. Anyone who reads and embodies these ideas will be greatly benefitted."

JAMES E. TRAPP,
President and CEO, Unity Worldwide Ministries

"Our words have the power to transform, bless, and empower us. In *How to Speak Unity*, Temple Hayes explains these wonderful truths in everyday language, so the words and their meanings enrich our lives. We are so blessed!"

KAREN DRUCKER,
Musician and Author of *Let Go of the Shore*

"For anyone who feels the hunger to know themselves gnawing at their souls, Temple Hayes serves up a five course meal! *How to Speak Unity* is a delicious and nourishing cookbook about life filled with recipes for blessings, energy, intuition and love. You'll want to savor every word!"

JANET BRAY ATTWOOD,
NY Times Bestselling Author of *The Passion Test*

"*How to Speak Unity* is a little gem. It is fitting that Temple Hayes write this book because she is a great spokesperson and the living embodiment of the Unity Principles."

PETER CALHOUN,
Hay House Author of *Soul on Fire*

HOW TO SPEAK
UNITY

By Temple Hayes

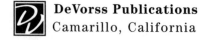

DeVorss Publications
Camarillo, California

How to Speak Unity
Copyright ©2011 by Temple Hayes

Library of Congress Control Number: 2011920295
ISBN13: 978-0-87516-859-3
FIRST PRINTING, 2011

DeVorss & Company, Publisher
P.O. Box 1389
Camarillo CA 93011-1389
www.devorss.com

Printed in the United States of America

WHAT IS UNITY?

Unity is a positive, practical, progressive approach to spirituality based on the teachings of Jesus and the power of prayer. Unity honors the universal truths in all religions and respects each individual's right to choose a spiritual path.

Unity was founded in 1889 by Charles and Myrtle Fillmore. The world headquarters in Unity Village, Missouri is located 15 miles southeast of downtown Kansas City. Established over 100 years ago, it became the spiritual headquarters for the world-wide Unity movement. Today the Mediterranean-style campus still offers a quiet refuge and nurturing activities for body, mind and spirit.

5 Basic Unity Principles

1. There is only One Power and One Presence active in the universe and all life, God, the Good, Omnipotent.

2. Our essence is of God; therefore, we are inherently good. This God essence was fully expressed in Jesus, the Christ, and is equally expressed in us.

3. We are co-creators with God, creating reality through thoughts held in mind.

4. Through affirmative prayer and meditation, we connect with God and bring out the good in life.

5. Through thoughts, words and actions, we live in the truth we know.

WHO WE ARE

We are not Unitarians.
We are not Unitarian Universalists.
We are Unity.

Unity exists to awaken every man, woman and child to their spiritual magnificence. Unity focuses on the common threads of all religious and spiritual practices, rather than the differences. We are all longing for a true recognition of the spirit within us. We do not teach you that we have *the* answer, we are showing you that you have *your own*.

Each Unity center and spiritual community – through Sunday celebrations, accredited Unity classes, seminars, and self discovery classes – provides both a spiritual and educational process in a supportive environment, enabling all who desire to discover the ultimate oneness and unity of life. Every Sunday morning at my service we perform the following song that clearly states who we are in Unity.

Welcome to This Place

Written by Temple Hayes and Christine Stevens

Copyright 2010

Here we are, in God's grace
Seeing love on every face
Holding hands, greeting eyes
No longer needing… to be disguised.

Let it go, at the door
Don't hold on anymore.
Changing times, new and old
Moving forward, brave and bold.

Welcome to this place of love and light
One Presence, One Power
Welcome to this place of loving life

Here we are, heart to heart
Knowing now is where you start.

Know the truth…that sets you free
Life has been waiting for you and me.
Welcome to this place of love and light.

One Presence, One Power
Welcome to this place of Loving Life.

One of the most rewarding aspects of being a Unity minister is when I meet individuals who seek a deeper under-standing of Unity. As they try to see their reality from a different perspective, their questions tend to challenge our beliefs and values. This not only gives me a chance to discuss the Unity philosophy, but it also forces me to look at the world from a different perspective, one that broadens my appreciation of how universal Unity really is. From all of the people I have met along my personal spiritual path, it's clear to me that the world is longing for compassion, direction and oneness. Here are some examples of these questions that perhaps you may have pondered at one time.

How can we use our crises and challenges to make a difference?

How can we answer human problems unless we are open to a higher knowledge and power?

....

If we were capable of answering the problems by ourselves, would we not already have done so?

How can we be one with others when we ourselves lack unity and understanding?

This book is a resource to understanding the spiritual language of life and the presence of Unity within us and all around us. This book can offer compassion, direction and oneness for you, your families, your communities and your world.

On the following pages you will discover both the words that are most often used while discussing Unity Principles, and ways to share the wisdom of these words. We believe our words are powerful and have the capacity to create what we believe in our lives.

....

The definitions are offered as tools to better help explain Unity, and enhance one's ability to communicate with others. Communication is the key to building a strong, spiritual life.

Our goal in discussing our beliefs with others is to inform and educate. Knowledge is powerful, and one of the keys to personal freedom and oneness.

Your dreams are waiting on you to come true. Awaken to your divine magnificence.

Loving life,
Temple Hayes

TOPIC LIST

ABSOLUTE	ENERGY	OMNIPOTENCE
ABUNDANCE	ETERNAL	OMNIPRESENCE
AFFIRMATIONS	EVIL	OMNISCIENCE
ATONEMENT	FEAR	PRAYER
BEING	FORGIVENESS	PRINCIPLE
BELIEFS	GOD	PUNISHMENT
BETTER AND BEST	HEALING	REALITY
BIBLE	HEAVEN	REALIZATION
BLESSINGS	HELL	REINCARNATION
CAUSE AND EFFECT	I AM	RELATIVE
CHAPLAIN	IMMORTALITY	RELIGION
CHRIST	INTUITION	RESURRECTION
CHRISTIAN	JESUS	SACRED
CO-CREATION	JUDGMENT	SAVIOR
CONSCIOUSNESS	KARMA	SCIENCE OF LIFE
CULT	LAW	SIN
DEATH	LIFE	SOUL
DEMONSTRATION	LOVE	SOURCE
DESTINY	MANIFESTATION	SPIRIT
DEVIL	MEDITATION	SPIRITUALITY
DIAGNOSIS	METAPHYSICS	THOUGHT
DISEASE	MIND	TRUTH
DIVINE ORDER	NAMASTE	UNIVERSE
DOCTORS-MEDICINE	NATURE	WORD OF GOD
DUALITY	NEW AGE	
EMBODY	NEW THOUGHT	

Is "Absolute" another word for God?
Yes.

....

The absolute truth is: God is the only presence and power in the universe. God is good all the time, and all the time, God is good. God is law, and law is God. God is love and love is God. As absolute being, God is unlimited, unconditional, infinite, impersonal, yet personal in all relationships. God is self-existent and all self-sufficient. God is principle existing in all things.

There is no "spot" where God is not. There is no place without God's grace.

Goodness is all around us, let us open our hearts to see it.

....

In Matthew 6:25, Jesus urges us to not be concerned about the clothes we shall wear or the food we shall eat. We know abundance is all around us, and as we open ourselves to it our good will come in. When we pray for our blessings, we are saying to our unlimited God, "I am ready to receive."

As we awaken spiritually, we begin to pay attention to everything that comes across our paths; the conversations, the gifts, and the surprise encounters are all evidence of the good which flows like a river into our lives.

Do we believe that our words have power?

People often think of affirmations as glorified "positive thinking." In Unity, we believe the words we declare to be our truth *become* our truth. As we grow spiritually, we become more aware of the words we use to define ourselves. We become sensitive to the seeds we are planting in our daily lives.

The words "I am" have the power to shape our lives; therefore, what follows "I am" needs to be what we are seeking to become and not a reinforcement of the negative patterning and conditions we are leaving behind. Like a glass of water which has become stagnant, it may take several pitchers of pure water to dilute the stagnation and return the water to its purest state. Positive affirmations change our lives and bring us to our purest state of being if we are willing to use them all the time and for as long as it takes.

What is atonement?

....

In traditional Christianity, atonement is the reconciliation of sinful men and women to God through the death of Jesus. In Unity, we do not recognize a need to be reconciled with God because we are all created in God's image and likeness. As human beings we are the microcosm of the macrocosm, created to express our unique magnificence in this life.

Pain and suffering comes from the refusal or unwillingness to express such magnificence, rather than as a result of sin. (see Sin)

Are we human beings or "human doings"?

In our culture, we have created a belief that levels of busyness equal levels of importance. To achieve this sense of importance, we often push ourselves past our natural limits. We were created as human beings rather than "human doings."

It is imperative that we remember to take time to simply be. Incorporating regular routines such as meditation or walks in nature rejuvenate our spirits and lower our stress. Nature is free to us and allows us to connect with our inner stillness. Psalms 46:10 reminds us to "BE still and know I am God."

In this space of stillness, we are able to relax and let go. There is tremendous power in letting go of what could be, for it is then we are able to accept what is. Somewhere between the thoughts of what could be and what is, there is usually a more perfect solution waiting to be birthed. Our greatest insights come from stillness.

Do you question your beliefs?
Do you know your beliefs?

. . . .

Jesus said, "It is done unto you as you believe." (Matthew 9:29) Many people use this quote yet do not know what it means.

Many people often go through their lives and never question what they believe. They have adopted the beliefs of their family, friends or communities. If you want to know what you believe, look at your life.

True happiness comes to individuals who understand that life responds to their own beliefs.

If you have loving relationships, you believe in your

own inherent goodness. If you are successful, you believe in your own worthiness. If you are blessed and know you are, you have developed a belief that God is everywhere present and good is everywhere around you.

Do we believe yesterday was better
than today? No.
We believe the best is yet to come.

Life is forever unfolding and ever changing. Evolution
implies that the change coming will be for the better.
Reverend Jack Boland, former Unity Minister in Detroit,
stated, "Don't ever let your good be the enemy of your best."
We often settle because we want to stay comfortable and
we're determined to keep things the same. We resist the
natural flow of life—for life is change. In holding on to the
good, we often miss opportunities to experience the
amazing. If we are not open to the possibilities around the
corner, we may only realize a small fraction of our potential.

Unity urges us to continue to seek new paradigms in which our joys and our good can continue to evolve and expand. Life, unlike an airplane trip, is not focused on the arrival or destination. Life is about the journey.

Do we use the Bible? You bet we do!
Do we take it literally? No.

The Bible is the result of God expressing through the minds and hearts of individuals with their own interpretations. In traditional Christianity, the Bible is taken literally word for word. There can be challenges with this. If we take the Bible literally, we must take every sentence as truth. If this is the case, every verse must apply and we cannot handpick the ideas we support with favoritism.

In Unity, we believe that when we read the Bible with an open mind, it is filled with great stories, parables and metaphors. We establish true love and appreciation of the

Bible when we apply the stories practically to our everyday lives. Truth is only truth to us when we use it. It will not influence us unless we understand it in a way which touches our minds and hearts and inspires us to be better people.

"We are so blessed, we are so blessed, we are so grateful for all that we have."

KAREN DRUCKER, SONGWRITER

Charles Fillmore, co-founder of Unity, stated in his book, *Mysteries of Genesis,* that, "Those who have a living faith in God's all-sufficiency do not beg or accept things without recompense but give value received for everything."

Imagine what the world would be like if everyone would give us value for everything we received. Each day when we rise, we are offering a blessing of thanks that we are alive. When we bless our work, we are grateful that we have a way in which to create in this life. When we bless our relationships, our family, and our friends, we are affirming our gratitude to God for creating their presence in our lives. When we bless our food, we acknowledge our oneness with it while also recognizing all the necessary events it took in order for us to enjoy it. Each time we bless anything, we acknowledge God's presence in everything.

How do I use the law of cause and effect?
How do I know it is working?

When a person plants a seed, the seed will grow. It is not necessary to dig the seed up to know it is growing. The seed does not question its purpose and will develop according to the laws of nature.

Likewise, what we focus upon grows in our lives. Cause is always the seed that will produce an effect in our lives. From a metaphysical perspective, we are always experiencing the effects of our thinking and deep-rooted beliefs (see Beliefs). Our conscious mind affirms ideas into our subconscious mind throughout the course of our day. What the conscious mind knows, the subconscious mind grows. The reality we see is the result of seeds we have planted in the past. As we awaken, we begin to change how we are thinking (the cause) so we may change what we see in our lives (the effect). The law is always working—even if we say it is not working, it proves itself by not working for us.

What is the role of a chaplain?

In Unity, the role of a chaplain is to support the spiritual community. A chaplain serves the ministry in pastoral care and acts as its arms to the congregation. The role of chaplain is one of the best trainings for anyone seeking spiritual growth. Due to our human conditioning, we want to fix things. However a chaplain is taught to listen lovingly without giving advice, to hold sacred space, and to keep all things confidential.

A chaplain prays for divine right action and outcome in all situations, creating sacred understanding and deepening of faith and oneness in God. A chaplain states "what" and allows God to express "how." What a wonderful opportunity to strengthen our belief that God knows what to do and how to do it.

Who is the Christ? Jesus is the Christ.
Will there be others? Hopefully...you.

· · · · · · · · · · · · · · · ·

It is really important to realize that "Christ" was not a last name for Jesus the person, but a way of expressing his consciousness. The word *Christ* is a title given to Jesus as he recognized his own full, divine potential. The word *Christ* originates from the Greek word *Christos*, which means "the enlightened one."

In Unity, Jesus was not the exception but the example for all of us. He is our way-shower, teacher and brother. He urged all of us to develop a relationship with God the way he did. We can express and appreciate our humanity, and at the same time work towards our own enlightenment. We are here to discover our divine potential and experience oneness. (see Consciousness)

HOW TO SPEAK UNITY

What do we say when asked if we are Christians?

....

In Unity we answer "yes" in the practical sense, and "no" in the traditional sense. We teach practical Christianity, meaning we apply the principles in which Jesus expressed himself as the Christ. We practice these messages daily. We may be the only Bible someone will ever know, and it is through our message and how we walk our talk they will seek a greater life.

We practice unconditional love, compassion, non-judgment, forgiveness, diversity, and acceptance within all of humanity.

We do not consider ourselves to hold the same beliefs as traditional Christians, because we do not believe in sin and atonement or that anything can separate us from God. We neither believe that God loves some countries more than others nor does God love some religions more than others. We are all children of God, innately divine; therefore, none of us need to be saved. We need to know the truth of loving God and loving life.

(see Atonement and Sin)

God is all of me, yet I am not all of God.

....

If God is our creator and we are made in the image and likeness of God then we have all the inherent qualities of God. God is the ultimate Creator and we are co-creating each and every moment of our lives by our thinking and feeling capacities.

In Unity, we are using prayer as intention, imagery as visualization, and meditation as direction in co-creating the life of our dreams.

When we are working with the laws of life, we know we are capable of co-creating the life we are seeking. We are prosperous first and foremost because we accept an infinite and prosperous God.

We co-create as we continue to grow in God knowing God is always greater than we are. In Unity, we affirm boldly, there is a Power for Good and we can use it.

What is consciousness?
Is it available to all of us?

Our consciousness is that to which we pay attention. It is our mental awareness. It can be defined as both the conscious and the subconscious mind and all they embody. Our consciousness is simply everything we have ever believed and accepted to be the truth about ourselves.

We have been told *who* we are and *how* to think all of our lives. We can change our consciousness by adding new ideas such as affirmative prayer and meditation. We begin to add new beliefs into our consciousness as we learn *how* to think for ourselves.

Our new beliefs attract greatness into our lives. The ultimate embodiment of consciousness is knowing God is good all the time.

Why do some people call Unity a cult?

Sometimes within our society, we label things we do not understand using words we do understand. Some family members may worry that we are part of a cult. Instead of becoming upset, this can become an opportunity to share truth. People are sometimes afraid of the unknown, especially if it challenges the outdated beliefs they have been told are true.

A cult is defined as "a religion regarded as unorthodox." Some may call Unity unorthodox, as it does not conform to the established doctrine of conventional Christianity. Unity challenges us to reexamine our beliefs and gives us the tools to identify them.

In Unity, we do not worship a person, place or thing. We believe that all of us are manifestations of God and we have direct access to pray, practice and participate with God on a moment to moment basis. We do not require a "middle person" or an agent to connect us with the Divine who created us.

Do we believe in death?

Spiritually speaking, no one can ever die. It is not possible, as on the most basic level, we are energy and energy is not capable of dying. Within the principle of life, there can be no death. We know we will die a physical death at some point, and we know it is not the end of our selves. Physical death is a transition during which we exchange our physical energy form for another form of energy.

However, we may die while we are physically still alive if we are not choosing to live fully in every moment. Often if we want to avoid death, we may also avoid truly living. We may die energetically and psychologically long before we die physically. Or we may choose to allow parts of ourselves to die, as stated in Jungian psychology, in order that our greater selves may live.

In Unity, we are more concerned with truly living because we know death is not the end for us, it is a new beginning. Life is spiral in nature, forever evolving, as are we.

*What do we mean by our ability to
demonstrate our good?*

The demonstration of our good is evident through the
laws of life which are always working. We have the ability
to demonstrate and measure our good by being able to see
and create what we desire. Many people do not believe
they can have what they desire; therefore, they do not ask
for what they truly want. They believe that to gain their
desires they must rely upon themselves and their limited
resources rather than asking God. We say in Unity, "we ask
what and leave the how up to God." How big is our
demonstration? How big is our belief and how strong is
our faith in God?

An interesting story of demonstration happened several years ago. A woman desired a piano—she wanted a Steinway Grand and did not want to pay anything for it. She asked me to affirm with her that she would attract the right piano at the right price. Three weeks later, she went to a concert and the master of ceremonies announced they had a piano which they only used for 4 days of the year, and they were searching for someone to store it the other 361 days of the year. You bet, it was a Steinway Grand.

As we celebrate our good, we have more to experience and enjoy. Through demonstration, we practice our principles and change our lives. (see Principle)

Do we believe in a predetermined destiny?

The only destiny we have is the one we declare as our own truth. If someone told us that we are never going to amount to anything and we affirm it all of our lives, it becomes our fulfilled destiny. We are given free will and choice as human beings and we have the ability to change our path at any crossroad.

We all have our own GPS (God Personalized System) in which to obtain our own success and spiritual magnificence. Our destiny is equal to the way we use cause and effect in our lives and how we expand our consciousness to attract our greater good. (see Cause and Effect and Consciousness) Our words are our magical wands, powered by our affirmations, that create the destiny of our choosing.

Do we believe in the devil?

Devil is the word L-I-V-E-D spelled backward. We do not believe the devil is a being in charge of evil or the forces of darkness. Rather the devil is the consequences of our own error choices when we have not L-I-V-E-D for our good. When we live in our pasts, we are "tempted" to convince ourselves that this is the way life is supposed to be. In most cases, our lack of honesty to ourselves is the devil which gets in the way of our highest good.

We believe there is only one power and presence in the universe, a power for good, and yet we can use this power to do destructive and negative things. We can easily sabotage our own good by repeating unhealthy patterns.

Beyond the five senses, we have gifts of imagination, perception and intuition. When we are "going against the grain," we are giving in to lower vibrations, rather than growing into our spiritual magnificence.

What do we do with a diagnosis?

Even though people every day are awakening to their own inner knowing, we are still part of a culture which wants to be told what to do. "Tell me the answer, and tell me I will be okay." Many people want their priest or rabbi to tell them what to do or their doctor to tell them what their results are going to be.

A diagnosis is a fact yet not necessarily a spiritual truth. It is one of many answers in order for a person to work towards the wholeness of their physical being. Within the intelligence of God, there is wholeness. (see Disease, Prayer and Doctors) .

What is dis-ease?

A disease prompted Myrtle Fillmore to pursue a balanced life, and this pursuit led to her healing and the birth of the Unity Movement. Though diagnosed with tuberculosis, she would say repeatedly, "I am a child of God; therefore, I do not inherit disease."

As children of God, we do not have to accept the human race conditioning which says we will inherit or adopt the same aches and ailments common among our family members.

We focus on spiritual truths rather than statistics and facts. The facts help to guide us, yet they do not necessarily define us. We can choose to receive a diagnosis of a disease as a helpful guide to our spiritual alignment. Through this understanding, we can then be still and find a better way of living. (see Diagnosis and Being)

DIVINE ORDER

The term "Divine Order" sounds almost scientific. What is it?

....

Divine order is scientific and is evident as the Universal Mind flowing through all things. We learn through life's lessons and experiences that everything is happening right here and right now as it is supposed to happen. We participate with Divine order by using declarations and affirmations to influence events, circumstances and conditions in our world.

Divine order, however, does not excuse our responsibility to show up on time, be present, and give our personal best. We are often in situations outside of our control; stuck in a traffic jam, waiting for a late shuttle or held up at the grocery line. When these events occur and we allow ourselves to experience them without resisting the flow, we are able to discover the reasons we were delayed. For example, following the news of a plane crash, we often hear stories about how a delay elsewhere caused others to miss the tragic flight, resulting in spared lives. Sometimes a moment or an event can change us forever for the better if we let it be. Divine order is always present and we can learn from it.

How do we perceive doctors and medicine?

In Unity, we take our good wherever we can find it. We bless doctors and the value they bring to society. We understand the value of doctors and medicine, yet they are not always the first and only answer.

We honor the spirit within and understand metaphysically that if the physical body is out of alignment there are other necessary parts of us which need our attention. Our mental body (thinking), our emotional body (feeling), our physical body (belief) and our spiritual body (inner truth) are all necessary parts of ourselves as we are healed and come into our own peace and oneness.

It is common in Unity to see students pursing many alternative paths to wholeness such as acupuncture, chiropractic care, and homeopathy.

How do we view the idea of duality?
There isn't one.

. . . .

Spiritual duality is the belief in two opposing powers—good and evil—rather than one. In Unity, we believe there is only one presence and power in the universe, God the good, the omnipotent. The belief in any other power is a false belief of separation, and as expressions of God, we can never be separate from our source.

We connect to God through prayer and meditation, and begin to live each day to see the good in all things. We look beyond appearances and know the presence of God is in all things, conditions and circumstances. When we affirm the presence of God is in all things, we not only discover it but learn to expect it. This concept, though easy to understand, requires commitment and dedication for us to embody it as common practice. (see Evil)

EMBODY

*What is embodiment and how do
we use it?*

....

When individuals embody a concept or a truth (see Truth), it becomes part of them. However, just because someone knows something intellectually, that does not mean the idea is integrated within their essence and consciousness.

We start today where we are, and as we integrate new ideas into our awareness and change our consciousness, we become the very thing we desire.

When we are telling students of life the truth, they may or may not be embodying the teachings. Similar to the famous analogy, "Give a man a fish and he'll eat for a day; teach him to fish and he'll eat for a lifetime," we know when students begin to embody a teaching. When students reveal a new awareness, they are embodying the concepts.

Is God's energy and ours the same? Yes!

Divine energy is present in everything... from the ocean to the tallest tree, from the smallest blade of grass to a human being. All is energy, and all is God substance and God essence.

Quantum physics tells us energy is working from the very edge of the universe to within the subatomic level. Energy is God expressing in, through and all around us. Energy is creative and given freely to those who allow it.

Why do we lack energy? We have self-imposed limits within our belief system which are holding many false beliefs about our age, our bodies and our physical beings. When we want more energy, we simply need to express more of God in, through and around us. There is an infinite amount of energy available to us, and if we are willing to change our beliefs, we will align with the truth (see Truth), and make wise choices in our physical and spiritual realities.

What is eternal life?

Eternal life is available to all of us as children of God and expressions of our Creator. If God is our creator and we are made in the image and likeness of God, then we have all the inherent qualities of God.

God is eternal with no beginning and no end. God is beyond measure, infinite and without time and space. Our soul is eternal and will never die. (see Death and Reincarnation)

Living energy can never die, though its form may change. No one really knows the form or essence our soul takes after it leaves this physical plane, yet we know by faith and through our life experiences that we are eternal.

"We are not human beings having a spiritual experience. We are spiritual beings having a human experience."

PIERRE TEILHARD DE CHARDIN

Why do people give power to evil?

....

A lack of understanding of the laws of life creates confusion regarding evil. When things which appear to be bad happen, we long for something or someone to blame. We blame people's wrong choices on the idea of being influenced by evil. Evil is the word L-i-v-e spelled backwards. (see Devil) When we live without listening, and do not acknowledge the internal and external signs all around us, we are misusing the power of God which is available to us. We are using our magnificent abilities as creative spirits to do wrong things.

Once we understand how evil expresses in our lives, we have the choice to be free from it. As we sow, we shall reap. Our negativity and lower vibrational thinking can bring about the misuse of power in our lives.

We are held accountable for the things we know to be right, moral and ethical, yet are not doing. We are not people being "done unto," we have the power of choice. It is a simple lesson in cause and effect. (see Cause and Effect; Vibration)

*What is the reason for fear and how
do we let go of it?*

Very simply stated fear is the absence of love. (see Love) Fear
is the feeling that we are separated from our Source. The
way out of fear is to focus upon love and gratitude.
FEAR = False Evidence Appearing Real.

Most facts fueled by negative thinking can create situations which appear to be real. When we turn away from
the fear and turn to God, we know there is nothing to be
afraid of because we know nothing can separate us from
God. Many people live out another acronym for fear:
Former Experience Actually Repeating.

When we react to a present situation based upon past
experience we may be fearful of a similar outcome.

Instead, when we operate from a sacred consciousness of new possibilities we do not need to let our emotions guide our outcome. Now is the greatest moment there is and all things are possible for those who love God. (see Sacred)

Why do we need to forgive?

Resentment gets re-sent and re-sent in our lives. When we hold discord in our bodies towards someone else, we are affected spiritually, mentally, emotionally and physically. Often, the lack of forgiveness contributes to the lack of abundance and creativity in our lives.

Forgiveness is the opportunity FOR GIVING to ourselves in a much greater way, versus holding anger and energy that takes away from our good. In Unity, we believe forgiveness in not a special event which happens every now and then. It is a way of living life every day. We end the day with a prayer of forgiveness for any moment in that day in which we showed any behavior which was less than the expression of our Christ consciousness.

When we forgive others, we remove the blocks of resentment and allow more good to flow into our lives. When we forgive ourselves, we take responsibility for our actions and step further into our spiritual magnificence.

*God is all there is and
all there is...is God.*

God is our Creator, Divine Intelligence, Sacred Energy, Higher Power and is available to all of us all of the time. In traditional religions, God and humanity are separated. In Unity, God is not a person but a principle, not a judge but an infinite power. As long we think of God as a person we will restrict God to personal limitations.

We are each an expression of God on this physical plane. God is impersonal yet personal to all who are open to the spirit within. We teach that it does not matter what name we give to God, what matters is what we believe about God.

In prayer we speak to God, and in meditation God speaks through us. God is love, wisdom, power, substance and most of all infinite possibility. All things are possible to those who claim God and accept God as their source. As we learn to honor our Creator of Life, we emerge into our divine magnificence and discover our wholeness. What our world needs now is a spiritual evolution where people realize the absence of God means the absence of life.

(see Life)

How can faith heal?

....

In John 5:5 and 6, Jesus asks, "Do you want to get well?" He later states "It is our faith which has made us well." These two profound truths, our *wanting* and our faith, are significant in our Unity teachings and can apply to everyone.

In the first truth, we acknowledge that we must *want* to be well. Some people find comfort from the compassion and attention a victim receives. This may distract them from the healing process. So to them, the benefits of being sick and helpless outweigh the idea of being well. In cases like these, their subconscious intention must continually strive for health and wellbeing.

In the second truth, we acknowledge that our faith plays an immense part in our ability to be whole. The faith we have in our doctor, our practitioner, our diagnosis (see Diagnosis) and our God is vital as we enter into the journey of healing.

Healing does not always refer to the correction of a physical or emotional condition, or reflect that we are somehow broken. Healing can be as profound and as simple as a new awareness of how to love in a greater way, or how to give more to our society. Healing is often a new insight.

In Unity, we know we are healed because we want to be and desire to be; however, we do not use metaphysical malpractice against or towards anyone. If students of Unity die of diseases we do not view this as a failure to want healing, or as a lack of faith. Rather it is part of our life process.

What do we believe about heaven?

In Unity, we believe heaven is a state of consciousness which is realized by living in the present moment. We do not acknowledge heaven in the traditional sense, as a place in the sky or a piece of property with pearly gates where all "good" people will one day coexist. It does not seem fathomable to us that we would reconnect with many people whom we did not have a great relationship with in the first place. A magical new place will not bring us closer to relationships anymore than a vacation can heal the "family."

Heaven is our gift when we learn to have a true relationship with ourselves and God. Heaven is given to each of us when we decide to allow our hearts and minds to be open and immerse ourselves in the good which is evident all around us. Instead of believing Heaven is No-Where, we affirm Heaven is Now-Here!

What do we believe about hell?

. . . .

Hell, like heaven, is a state of mind. Hell is not a place of
fire and brimstone destined for certain people as punishment for the way they have chosen to live. A person who
experiences hell on earth believes in two powers rather
than one.(see Duality)

A heart which closes during a life of resisting "what is,"
and which refuses to see the potential of what can be, is a
heart of separation. As long as people resist "what is," they
feel disconnected from God and from the infinite possibilities which are available to all people. When people feel that
life is being done "unto them", they experience hell in
everyday life.

Important note: Though in Unity, we do not believe in a physical heaven or hell, we believe in consequences. (see Cause and Effect) We live a spiritual life not because of what "may one day" happen to us. We live a spiritual life because there is no other way to live life fully.

I am that which I state I am.

. . . .

In Exodus 3:14, God said to Moses, "I am who I am." "I am" is an expression of God, and what we affirm by using the "I am" becomes our truth. We are the unique micro of the macrocosm. As we expand our ability not to set things right but to see them right, we are able to see beyond any appearance of separation.

God's name is on everything. When we affirm with an open heart the "I am" within us, we are able to see the "I am" within all people, through all things and within all of nature. We are able to let go and let God, and though we do not understand what we see with human eyes, we believe that ultimately all is well. God is everywhere present in all things, conditions and circumstances.

What does it mean to be immortal?

By definition, *immortal* means "remembered or celebrated through all time." In Unity, Easter is the celebration of immortality. Our way-shower, Jesus, showed us that living people never die. We are celebrated and remembered through all times.

In describing the incomparable beauty of immortality, Ralph Waldo Emerson states, "Friendship, like the immortality of the soul, is too good to be believed."

If we believe in the infinite nature of God, and we believe that we are made in the image of God, then we, too, must be immortal. We are mirrors of God; therefore, though our physical being changes, our existence does not. (see Death and Resurrection)

We have intuition, nature has instincts.

....

Many people ask today, "How can my life be more magical?" and "How can I go from ordinary to extraordinary?" Great thinkers have taught us that we either go through life learning and struggling, or we listen to our own intuition. Each of us has the innate ability to listen to our inner voice and receive guidance for direction, clarity or choices. When we develop trust that our intuition works for us, we expand our active use of it.

How many times have we said to ourselves, "Wow, I wish I would have listened to that hunch or that feeling." Intuition is a crucial part of spirituality, because when we pray for answers or meditate for guidance, the answers come. Whether we heed our intuition or not is an expression of our free will.

Who is Jesus?

In his book *Christian Healing*, Charles Fillmore states "Jesus was Himself a parable. His life was an allegory of the experiences that man passes through in developing from natural to spiritual consciousness." We all aspire to develop our spiritual consciousness like he did. He assured us that while he was able to do great things, we would do even greater. (John 14:12)

Many of us who have discovered Unity were longing for a spiritual community which truly practiced the teachings of Jesus. These ideas include yet are not limited to unconditional love, diversity, forgiveness, and the love of

God rather than the fear of God. We focus on living and obtaining the qualities of his message. It is his life that changes us, rather than his death. Jesus embodied the Christ which lives in us, as us, and through us. (see Christ)

Do we accept judgment as part of our teachings?

"Judge not, that ye be not judged," (Matthew 7:1) is a simple scripture we can state as a mantra, yet have difficulty following. The first phase is to understand what judgment is *not*. Judgment is not the same as discernment. We say, "Do not allow your spirituality to replace your common sense." God has blessed us with wisdom.

When we use discernment in a situation, we are working with facts and truth to make the best choice for all concerned. Jesus declared this as right thinking. When we judge, we decide that others have not made the right choice, and self righteously we feel we are divinely capable of guiding their directions.

"Judgments prevent us from seeing the good that lies beyond appearances."

WAYNE DYER

How do we explain karma?

Karma, in popular terms means that in this lifetime or in other lifetimes, a soul has made certain choices, and karma is the consequences of those choices.

In Unity, we believe that we are working with the law of cause and effect. (see Cause and Effect) When we recognize our mistakes and realize that our mistakes are creating consequences, we are healed. There is not a record book keeping track of the number of "good" or "bad" actions we take. Karma's effect ends once our awareness is brought to wholeness.

The knowing of the law becomes the practice of the law which leads to results. Jesus wanted us to understand how to pray by declaring to God, give us THIS DAY our daily bread and forgive us as we forgive others. This is living in the consciousness of using cause and effect on a daily basis. In the schoolroom of life we learn to do better; therefore, we create better results in our lives.

*The law of life is always at work —
whether you realize it or not.*

If you recall the song "I Fought the Law," originally
recorded by Sonny Curtis and The Crickets in the 60's,
you're probably already singing the chorus to yourself right
now — *I fought the law and the . . . law won. I fought the law
and the . . . law won.* The lyrics of this simple song may
seem stark, but the underlying message comes through
loud and clear in metaphysics and Unity. The chorus
reminds us of the initial steps we take when learning about
the principles of Unity and the Law of life.

There is an immutable law that is always working. The
Law of life is a law of growth and is always working. We
are constantly growing and we can't stop it. What we can

do is accept it and work with it. When we believe it, trust it, and commit to it, we are able to get amazing results. If we say the law does not work, it is actually still working for us but we don't recognize the direction of the growth and how it manifests in our lives. Many of us do not thoroughly understand how electricity works, yet we are able to turn on a light switch and benefit from the electric current. We do not have to understand physics and metaphysics fully in order to know that what we declare to be true in our lives will manifest—if it hasn't already.

It happens to us all from time to time. At the slightest disappointment, we may retreat and seek comfort in an unhealthy way, not realizing the Law is ALWAYS at work and pushing us to learn and grow. Remember, the Law of life is a law of GROWTH. So, the next time you find yourselves mentally fighting a new predicament with your old unhealthy thoughts, remember this...

I fought the law and the . . . law won.

> *"God, my life is your gift to me and what I do with my life is my gift to You."*

OG MANDINO

....

Life is a gift. It is given without instructions, directions, or an owner's manual. Life is a performance with no dress rehearsal and a great symphony with very few encores.

Some people have near death experiences, yet in Unity we focus more on the "near life" experiences. True living means giving all that we are and have to everything we do. Life mirrors the enthusiasm and commitment we bring to it. Loving people live in a loving world, lonely people live in a lonely world, and hostile people live in a hostile world. When we are asking life to give us something, we will receive it when we start to bring it our awareness. In other words, we get what we bring. The quality of life is not measured by the number of years but by the understanding that life happens *to us* by happening *through us*.

"All you need is love."

Lennon / McCartney

Love is the common thread among all living things. The energy of love is the great healer. Matthew 19:19 instructs us to "love thy neighbor as thyself." Many people are taught and believe it is wrong to love themselves and selfish to have their own best interest in mind. However, if we do not love ourselves, how can we truly care for someone else? Have you ever met people who despised themselves, did not take care of themselves, and yet loved everyone else? Probably not.

In Unity, we do not believe it is possible to think we can love other people unconditionally and want the best for them, unless we are practicing the same action of love within ourselves. We see ourselves in others not only from our eyes but from our hearts. When our hearts are filled with love, love is what our eyes will see.

Is manifesting supernatural?

It is our divine birthright to manifest various things in our lives. We say in Unity and in New Thought teachings that a thought plus a feeling equals an action. As we declare into the Universe with prayer and positive affirmations, we see those requests fulfilled in many forms. We tend to focus upon the four main areas of our lives; career and purpose, relationships, creative self-expression and abundance.

As I was working a few years ago on the idea of manifestation, the thought occurred to me that we can all have a PhD in metaphysics, with Prayer, Humility and Devotion. When we pray, we call in that which we desire in our lives. We remain humble as to how these wants and desires appear. And we remain devoted to God and knowing our prayers are always answered. The manifestation may not appear in a new job but could be a change in our current one, or we could change the way we feel about it.

We are all constantly manifesting. The question is, "What are we focusing on which causes what we see to come into being?" If we like what we see, wonderful! If we do not like our manifestations, then we need to change our focus.

MEDITATION

Is meditation important?

Meditation is essential to students of spirituality. To be still and know is one of our greatest assets in everyday life. Whether experiencing meditation while sitting with soft music, or walking in meditation near water or at the beach, we are connecting to nature and to ourselves in these moments.

Meditation further develops our ability to see inwardly and to remain peaceful inside regardless of outside circumstances. We draw from the wisdom that nothing can really happen *to* us, unless we allow it *to* happen through us.

Meditation is an amazing practice which clears the way for the "divine knowing" within all people. It creates a sacred space somewhere between what has happened and what is happening, allowing faith to reassure the spirit within. All is well, sings my soul. (see Nature, I AM, God, Being)

Is Unity a metaphysical teaching? What does that mean?

The journey of a metaphysician is the spiritual path in which God reveals all things, both in the physical world and beyond. *Meta* means "beyond," and *physical* is based upon the five senses. We know in Unity, we are working with the law and love of our good beyond the physical realm, and amazing miracles are part of every day life. (see Demonstration)

As a small child, I declared to my parents that I wanted a puppy, to which they said "no." I declared this same desire to God, and within a few days a puppy showed up at my door.

In Unity, we believe as the praises go up (as our vibration is lifted), the blessings come down. The more we celebrate the good which God brings to us, the higher our energy will be lifted beyond our own physical understanding. God is the creative intelligence and infinite life force in all of our affairs.

What do we mean by mind?

. . . .

We often affirm, "There is one life, that life is God and that life is our life right now." There is one mind and it is expressing in us, as us and through us. There is one power, one mind and one life in all that we see.

Just as the sun beams light in and around all things, mind is everywhere present. On the spiritual dimension, all of our minds are connected through the One. If something is happening to some of us, on some level it is happening to all of us. We are the tapestry of all that is and continues to be in the mind of God.

God (Mind) is forever evolving through all things. As we begin to allow new paradigms to emerge in our lives, our subconscious mind frees us from living in a box of limited ways of thinking. It is easier to understand mind in all things when we are able to expand our awareness of a dated archetype of God limited by human expectations into the discovery of a principle which is infinite. (see God)

What does "namaste" mean?

"The God within me meets and recognizes the God within you" is the basic meaning of the word *namaste*. Though we all seek different paths and adapt to our own unique beliefs, we are all made of the same energy and essence of God. Our life force as humans is the same.

We have discovered among indigenous people of the world, that though they lived in separate countries and did not have the means to communicate, they shared similar rituals. We have the immense ability to connect with the human heart beyond language and geographical borders. Often before there is a world-changing event, such as a tsunami or a major earthquake, we begin to feel anxious or perhaps weary.

When we practice namaste, we are often able to look beyond our differences and remember the color of our blood is the same. Namaste is oneness. If it is happening to you, it is happening to me…for in the essence of namaste, we are ONE!

Nature is our greatest teacher.

....

Alan Watts, a British philosopher, stated that we are not born *onto* the Earth, we are born *out of* the Earth. Therefore, nature is not separate and apart from us, it is part of our connectedness with life. We cannot exist as physical beings without the harmony and respect of and for nature.

Unity co-founders Charles and Myrtle Fillmore believed strongly in the elements of nature and how we are affected spiritually by being in the presence of God through nature. Both of them dedicated the majority of their lives to being vegetarians, though they were clear it was their own personal choices and not a Unity creed or expectation.

Unity Village rests on several hundred acres filled with full and lush gardens and ample wildlife. We cannot love God without being connected to all of God's creations.

Nature is not only who we are, it teaches us who we are becoming when we listen with respect and admiration.

What is the difference between New Age and New Thought?

....

When people are referring to New Age, they are usually speaking about crystals, astrology, magic cards, channeling, psychics and many other forms of wisdom which lend an additional perspective or give more information about their lives. These are all wonderful tools for students to express as opinions, to use for healing, or to reference as a map or guideline. We keep these tools in perspective and know they are showing us suggested possibilities for our lives.

In Unity and New Thought, we accept it is done unto us as we believe. Therefore, if we believe the rock will heal us, it will. If we believe the psychic is right, our belief will make it so. All of these tools are incredible, yet we know spirituality is never designed to replace common sense. Life is not a game of Simon Says, for no one has the truth for ourselves except ourselves and the Divine Wisdom within us.

At the end of every truth or opinion offered to us by outside sources, we still have the freedom of choice and the power of discernment to use regarding our outcome. (see Beliefs and Law)

What is the New Thought Movement?

Unity is part of a global movement known as the New Thought Movement. At its core, New Thought believes there is a common thread within all the world's religions and philosophies, "There is one Life, that life is God, and that life is our life right now." There is a power for good and we can use it.

New Thought was born over 150 years ago to provide oneness for global spirituality, rather than emphasize the distinctions of the dogmas among various religions of the world. There is a universal language, beneath all the layers of doctrines and creeds, which draws out of all people the longing to connect with something greater.

We do not believe that God loves some countries more than others or some churches more than others, otherwise God would be a person and life would have no order. (see God)

New Thought empowers individuals to learn *how to think* rather than forcing them into *what to think*. Our founders, Charles and Myrtle Fillmore sought to discover Unity within all forms of spirituality, therefore Unity emerged as not only our name but also our daily method, motto and mission.

What is the meaning of Omnipotence?

Omnipotence is another way of stating what we believe God to be. God is all powerful and all knowing.

As spiritual students in Unity, we begin to shift our thinking and love of God from a person who is in the sky, to a God which is an unlimited principle and who is all powerful.

When we can accept this vast and emerging definition of God, then we are able to see how our thoughts are prayers and we are always praying. The very act of prayer does not change God, it changes us. All of our prayers are heard because we know that God is all powerful and all knowing. We stop telling God how big our problems are, and begin telling our problems how big God is.

We listen and we accept our readiness for this immense power to work in all areas of our lives. God, the omnipotent power of the universe, is well capable of expressing amazing things through us. We let it be so!

What does the term omnipresence *mean and how does it affect me?*

God is everywhere present and always available. The very act of speaking about God seems to limit how incredible God truly is. God is in every thought, every word, everything physical and non-physical, seen and unseen. God is all that has ever been or will ever be. God is all of us and we are expressing that which we know and believe God to be.

Unity's core principle is "God is present in All things." The All is One Power, One Presence, One God expressing in and through each of us. One God expressing through and as all things. There is no place or spot where God is not.

In Unity we also say, "God is good all the time, and all the time, God is good."

As we approach our lives with the belief that God is present and good, we will get what we believe. We will retrain ourselves to see God's presence everywhere.

How is God omniscient?

Omniscience in its simplest form means "all knowing." If God is all powerful (omnipotent) and all present (omniscient), then God is also all knowing. God Mind is all and knows all. When we face situations and circumstances, we have the ability to open up to the omniscient grace of God and allow insight, direction and new truths to surface on our pathway. We open to these new awakenings and discoveries through prayer and meditation, which allow the space for new ideas to flow.

We can look at any situation or circumstance and declare, "There is an intelligence in the universe, God the omniscient, who knows the way and the means for this situation to result in a wonderful outcome." We know without hesitation or lack of faith that God knows all, and we let this knowledge flow through us. We are listening, God.

What is the meaning of prayer?

Prayer generally implies having spiritual communion with God or an object of worship, through supplication, thanksgiving, adoration, or confession. Often the undertone of prayer is pleading, bargaining and making amends with God. In Unity and New Thought, prayer is an affirmative declaration of things, events and circumstances which we are accepting as truth. In other words, we state in prayer that which we desire to see. Our prayers, when heard by others, have heartfelt responses because they are positive, inspirational, and affirmed as if the desire is so.

Prayer does not change God, prayer changes us. Our change is within our own minds and hearts in order to receive those things, events and circumstances we desire. In prayer, we only state the conditions we want. We do not put into the prayer the conditions we do not want. If someone is not well, the prayer is "thank you God for my health," rather than "heal my illness." (see Law and Manifestation) We believe God is omniscient, therefore we must also believe God already knows what we desire. Our prayers invite what we desire into being.

What are the values of our principles?

Principles are a set of standards or guidelines for our lives. They are the map we use to drive through life. In Unity, we say we have tools rather than rules, and these tools enable us to live with purpose and meaning. When we hear the word rule, we immediately want to break it, or we worry that we will. When we speak of tools or guidelines, we are empowering ourselves to live a life of deeper meaning.

(see the 5 Basic Unity Principles)

What is punishment?

Punishment is a human rule based upon a belief that we live in a universe which judges and scolds us. In her book *Your Hope of Glory*, Elizabeth Sand Turner suggests that Moses' Ten Commandments came from a perspective of "thou shalt not." The old laws implied that breaking these rules could result in punishment and even death.

As humanity evolved, Jesus came to teach about consequences in the Sermon on the Mount. When we are instructed "ye shall be blessed" if you apply this principle, then we understand the idea of cause and effect. We decide to choose our actions according to the consequences. (see Cause and Effect)

What is our reality?
Is it just another "reality" show?

. . . .

There is a wonderful quote from Shakespeare's *Hamlet*: "There is nothing either good or bad, but thinking makes it so." Many people label their experiences as good and bad, and these labels define their realities. Oftentimes they say, "This is just the way I am. This is my reality." People may get very comfortable with and accept what they have been told, or state that *what is* is all there will ever be in their lives.

Reality with a capital *R* is the absolute truth of God. Reality with a small *r* is that which we have labeled our truth. We are fortunate when the Reality of God and our reality go hand in hand. We can always change our reality if we are willing to draw from God's greater truth.

In other words, there will always be "facts" of living in the world, such as the real estate market or the economy, yet there is also truth. This truth is the wisdom of Jesus, to be in the world yet not of the world.

What is a realization?

. . . .

Miracles are described as what happens when we wake up one day and "we are there," we have achieved or arrived at a place in our lives we previously thought to be difficult or nearly unattainable. It seems to be a miracle because we do not recall all the necessary steps it took to get us there. A realization is when we have an awakening, or an Ah-Ha moment which will free us from an old paradigm of limitation and sorrow.

There is a saying: If we knew better, we would have done better. When we have a realization, we are able to do better because we are no longer in our own way. We begin to honor our own intuition and insights and do not resist the path of our divine nature.

Once we have a shift in our consciousness, we cannot return to a place of not knowing, for it will create pain and discomfort. Our GPS—God Personalized System—will support us in keeping on track as we continue along this incredible journey we call life.

What does Unity say about reincarnation?

Many Unity students on a spiritual pathway believe in reincarnation. They have too many moments in their lives, either within their careers or within their relationships, which seem very familiar.

Through centuries stories have been told of how people's souls long to reconnect. Though they come from many sides of the Universe and other lifetimes, their souls manage to find each other again.

Charles Fillmore states in his book, *Keep a True Lent*, the fact that we do not remember past lives proves nothing. As he explains, we also do not remember the day we were born but we do not question the fact of our birth.

However, we do take a realistic stance regarding rein-carnation, and know that everyone could not have been a famous person in a past life. We also understand that regardless of what we may have been or how we may have previously lived in past lives, we are accountable for who we are and how we live in this one.

What does "relative" mean in New Thought?

While we know there is only one presence and power in the universe, God the good, we also know God is relative. How we are able to establish a relationship with this All Knowing and All Loving God is relative to how we use our five senses, our experiences, our intuition and our perceptions. How we identify who God is to us is our relative relationship with the Divine.

As students of truth, what is relative or how we relate to God today, may be expanded in a moment or over time. As we are able to expand our consciousness, our relationship with God expands to include all of God's creations. We recognize the nature of all things relative to the one presence and one power, God.

How does Unity embrace religion?

Someone once said, "My mind is my church and what I believe is my religion." Our mind creates that which we focus on, becoming our truth and our church. What we believe is our religion because our beliefs create the world around us. Religion in its original intention was a good thing.

The word *religion* means to tie, fasten or bind. Religion was meant to create the unity of humankind with God.

The issue with religion is that it has become a "we are right, you are wrong" paradigm. Many people have been killed or disregarded due to religious misunderstandings, leading to very little unity. Some even promote the idea that God loves some beliefs more than others and some countries more than others.

Unity believes there are many paths to God and welcomes all people from all faiths and all walks of life. We do not attempt to be all things to all people, yet we want to teach people that God through them can do all things. Unity celebrates the common thread with all religious organizations, that there is One Presence and Power in the Universe.

What is the meaning of the resurrection?

....

In Unity, Easter is one of the most exciting times of the year. It represents new beginnings and our ability to "cross out" old ways of thinking and invite new ways into being. We often celebrate with a beautiful sunrise service, and declare that as Jesus has risen so have we risen to both a new awareness of the greatness of God, and our ability to express the Christ consciousness in our daily living. To us, the Easter story does not reflect death and redemption. Rather, it is a metaphor showing us that living people never die, for life is eternal.

The resurrection ritual allows each of us the opportunity to resurrect to a life of possibility and infinite wisdom and blessings.

We celebrate with excitement that Christ lives in each of us. (see Jesus and Christ)

HOW TO SPEAK UNITY

Everywhere we walk is sacred ground.

....

This is the greatest moment that you and I have ever lived.
We have never been better or greater than we are right now.
As long as we believe there was a better yesterday or that
tomorrow holds for us some great guarantee, we are missing
out on the greatest moment that we will ever have, and that
is *right now*. Right now is where we have the power to
change our minds, make a decision or let go of something
we no longer want in our lives, for we truly are empowered
individuals.

Empowerment means living a life of sacred value. Just
as God is evolving, so are we. We begin today. Right now is
where we start. We are standing on holy ground. Walk your
journey, treasure every moment and know your sacredness.

....

SAVIOR

Do we need a savior?

. . . .

The word *savior* implies someone is being rescued from
danger or harm. In traditional Christianity, Jesus died for
humankind's sins to save us from our "bad ways and wrong
doing." In this way of thinking, sin is the nature we are
born into through no choice or action of our own. From
birth, we are bad and undeserving people unless we accept
this doctrine as truth and are saved.

In Unity, there is nothing to be saved from. We are
born inherently good, created in the image and likeness of
God, with free will and choice in our lives. We can either
learn through intuition, insights and awareness, or through
trial and error.

The only subtle way in which Jesus "saves" us is through the awareness we receive from his teachings. He wanted us to enter into a place of believing in the new laws of life and connection to his father, our God.

In Unity, Jesus is our teacher and his teachings—not his death—"save" humanity when we incorporate the way he lived into our daily lives. We are saved when we are able to free ourselves from the harsh judgments of the world and become righteous thinkers with the innate ability to see things right. (see Christ, Sin, Jesus)

What role does science play in our lives?

Science simply means that a condition proves itself. Our lives prove to us each day that we are working within laws and principles, and the more we become in tune with these truths, the greater the magic expresses in our lives. The law of attraction is always working and is always proving itself to the mind of the beholder.

There are no accidents and no coincidences in our lives. Life doesn't just "happen" unless we have agreed to make it so. A loving person lives in a loving world, a thankful person lives in a thankful world, an angry person lives in an angry world and a victim always experiences reasons to be sorry.

It is our divine birthright to be a bright star in the universe and claim our greatness. We do not benefit anything or anyone by being small. Everything is happening because we are co-creating our reality with God.

Do we believe that human beings are sinful?

. . . .

Sin and guilt are both manmade ideas. Sin comes from the Greek word *hamartia,* an ancient archery term meaning "missing the mark." We all miss the mark from time to time. With the best of intentions, we still repeat old patterns, make the same choices which produce the same results, and limit our good by being closed-minded.

We do not sin, we make mistakes, and with every choice we make there are consequences. In the Bible we are told, "to him whom much is given, much is required." (Luke 12:48) In other words, when we know better and do it anyway, we experience consequences from those choices immediately.

There is a law operating in our lives that is directly measureable according to our personal levels of awareness. God does not punish us for our sins. As people, we must forgive our actions, and through forgiveness and awareness our lives work for the better. God is neither a coach with a scorecard nor an accountant keeping records. (see God)

Do we all have souls?

. . . .

God is the only presence and power in the universe. Each of us is an individualized expression of the One.

Our souls, like our fingerprints are unique. We each follow our unique paths, and our souls recognize the way of these paths.

Sayings like "that touched my soul," are mirrors of who we are as spiritual beings. From birth, our souls bring to our lives an intention of expression. Through the course of our lives, we find or attract experiences and events with nature and people which develop our paths toward fulfilling these intentions. When we do not listen to this inner guidance, we do not honor our lives. When we avoid the paths we are meant to follow, we experience soul frag-mentation and require support in order to return to our feelings of wellbeing and wholeness. People often come to Unity and remark they feel at home. In other words, their souls have received a gift of love and unconditional recog-nition. (see Absolute)

> *"God is my Source, God is my Power,*
> *God gives me everything I need."*
>
> KAREN DRUCKER, SONGWRITER

. . . .

Imagine what the world would be if everyone realized there is one source in the universe, the presence and power of their Creator. We often confuse our limited resources with our source of fulfillment. We may tend to think of our jobs as our source, our family inheritances as our source, or the love we receive from our relationships as the source of happiness.

However, we are all blessed with an infinite, unlimited Source which we cannot "out-give" or outlive in this lifetime. The more we use the gifts and talents with which

God has blessed us, the more gifts and talents we discover within our magnificent being.

When we think of our limited resources as our source, we become attached to them and often feel stagnant because we are unable to allow the greater good to manifest in our lives. (see Better and Best and Demonstration)

What is spirit?

Many people have grown up singing a song which says, "There is a sweet, sweet Spirit in this place and I know it is the Spirit of the Lord." The Lord, the Law, is always present. There is not a place where spirit does not exist.

Author and retired minister Raymond Charles Barker stated, "If God had any intention for us, it would be to leave us alone so we may discover ourselves." We discover the grace of spirit when we realize that our abilities are not limited by our personalities and our experiences. Principle is not bound by precedent. When we allow spirit to express through us, amazing gifts and talents emerge which exceed our imaginations.

This is what Jesus taught in John 14:10, "Don't you believe that I am in the Father, and that the Father is in me? The words I say to you are not just my own. Rather, it is the Father, living in me, who is doing his work."

There is a sweet spirit expressing through us, and as we allow it to exist we understand we are the individualized identity of spirit.

Can we be separated from our spirituality?

Religion tends to teach us "what to think" using various rules and spirituality tends to teach us "how to think" using various tools. Everything is spiritual, and we are spiritual beings. How we use the experiences of our lives, what we allow and what we accept becomes our spirituality.

Spirituality is the conscious decision to work with and demonstrate our principles in daily life. Spirituality requires our participation. In our findings as spiritual leaders, the most *involved* tend to be the most *evolved*.

We grow in our spirituality through our intention to practice "expressing the Christ" in all situations and circumstances. Our goal with our spirituality is not to be welcomed in a far away place or nirvana, but to experience heaven on earth by living a life of greatness while discovering the spirit within.

THOUGHT

What is thought?

....

"What we think about God, about ourselves, and about our neighbors does make a great difference in our daily lives. Through ignorance of our real selves and of the results of our thinking, we have let our thoughts flow at random. Our minds have been turned toward the external of our being, and nearly all our information has been gathered through our five senses. We have thought wrongly because we have been misinformed by these senses, and our troubles and sorrows are the results of our wrong thinking." Emilie Cady, *Lessons in Truth*, p. 30.

This is an incredible statement! When we can become trained thinkers and realize that our thoughts which are held in mind, create their own kind then we understand that life is not being "done unto us."

We have free choice and free will in how our thoughts are used.

How do we know what is true?

There is one truth which matters to us as students of life. The truth which we discover along our journey is the truth which is imperative to follow and honor.

Jesus stated this simple method to live by, "and you will know the truth, and the truth will set you free." (John 8:32) He did not say we shall all know the same truth nor did he say "set yourselves free" *and then* know the truth.

The path of joy is one in which we listen inwardly and follow the truths we believe. All of us are blessed with our own inner awareness of what actions or movements forward we are to take. As we follow what we know to be true, our lives prosper. As we deny the truths we are hearing, not only are we not free, we are limited to a life of trial and error. (see Jesus, Christ)

Describing the universe cannot define it.

. . . .

The universe is vast, infinite and beyond definition. Just when we think we are able to describe it either scientifically, astrophysically or qualitatively, we discover more. The Universe, reflecting the essence and power of God, continues to expand and to grow.

We cannot avoid or deny the effects of living in an infinite universe. It is more than our description of it, it is our acceptance that all things are possible with God. As God grows, we grow!

Throughout history, philosophers and geniuses have discovered amazing breakthroughs. As we continue to discover more of the infinite, growing God, we discover more of the infinite growth within ourselves.

How do we define the word of God?

....

The Bible begins in Genesis with God creating and naming all things. This is the original creative word, or thought, of being.

To us as metaphysicians, the word of God created the heavens and the earth, and our words have been creating ever since. Our greatest gift as expressions of God is the ability to state and declare into the universe that which we choose to create. The power of the word brings our desires and wants into manifestation.

Everything we declare and add to the "I am," we create and bring forth into our lives. (see Manifestation and I AM)

ABOUT THE AUTHOR

Temple Hayes is an ordained Unity minister and international motivational speaker. Reverend Hayes is currently CEO of First Unity Campus, a New Thought center, in St. Petersburg, Florida. First Unity Campus transcends all the religious denominations, embraces all ethnicities, and reaches beyond national borders.

Beyond her role as a spiritual leader, she is also a practicing shamanic healer, and an All-American softball player. Temple Hayes was elected to Outstanding Young Women of America in 1988; to the International Who's Who of American Professionals in 1997; to the American Biographical

Institute for Great Women of the 21st Century for 2006; and to the National Association of Professional Women in 2008. She has also been honored with the Footprints Award by the National Sigma Gamma Rho Sorority for outstanding community service.

To learn more about Temple and her purpose and passions in life, visit:

www.TempleHayes.org
www.templehayesspeaks.com

For more information about Unity, Please visit your local
Unity church or contact one of the following organizations:

Unity or Unity House Publications
1901 NW Blue Parkway
Unity Village, MO 64065-0001
816-524-3550
www.unity.org

Unity Worldwide Ministries
PO Box 610, Lee's Summit, MO 64063
816-524-7414
www.unity.org

Affiliated New Thought Network
522 Central Avenue
Pacific Grove, CA 93950
831-372-1159
www.newthought.org